A COLLECTION OF BUD NEILL'S POCKET CARTOONS

Selected and Introduced
by
Ranald MacColl

ZIPO
PUBLISHING

First published in Great Britain in 1997 by
ZIPO PUBLISHING LIMITED
4 Cowan Street, Glasgow, G12 8PF

website: www.zipo.co.uk
e-mail: info@zipo.co.uk

Corrected reprint 1997

ISBN 1 901984 01 X

A catalogue for this book is available from the British Library

Original cover design by Ranald MacColl

Printed and bound in Great Britain by The Cromwell Press, Wiltshire

CONTENTS

INTRODUCTION   5

THE WAR   11
THE RATIONS   21
GI BRIDES   29
FERRS PLEEZ   37
BAUCHLES, BAIRNS AND BAMS   45
NINE TO FIVE   61
DOON THE WATTER   69
SPORTSLINE   79
WEE WIMMEN AND WEE MEN   87
WIMMEN AND WEANS   101
MRS T   109
THE MESSAGES   117
LIPSTICK AND LUMBERS   125
TEDS   133
CAURS AND CLIPPIES   141
THE POLIS   149
ARRAFERR   157
FISH AND FAUNA   165
TERASSIN' AND TEARS   175
EXPRESS VIEWS   183

THE GENIE OF THE LAMP BLACK

INTRODUCTION

Mention Lobey Dosser to most inhabitants of the West of Scotland and a flicker of recognition will register in their eyes . . . "Yes, the wee Glasgow cowboy sheriff with the two-legged horse and the baddie - what's-his-name - Rank Bajin."

Most will be aware of the bronze statue dedicated to these cartoon characters; erected with funds from a popular public subscription. But those younger than thirty will probably draw a blank at the mention of the creator of the famously quirky Keelie Western cartoon tales.

Bud Neill's little eponymous hero was first published in 1949 to immediate popular acclaim. This was, however, no overnight success story for the cartoonist. Bud had already established a large following of *Evening Times* readers since his first pocket cartoon appeared five years previously in 1944.

He began his career in newspaper cartooning relatively late in life. At 33 he wrote a succinct and barbed reply to a series of complaints by passengers of the wartime buses in the "Letter to the Editor" section of a Glasgow newspaper. The Editor was intrigued and not a little suspicious that a bus driver could compose such an eloquent letter. A consequent investigation of the writer's credentials found him to be a legitimate transport worker. There followed a meeting at the Editor's office, where Bud mentioned that he could "draw a wee bit" and he was offered a job as a pocket cartoonist for the *Evening Times* on a piece-work basis.

It's the kind of wee fairytale that Fairy Nuff would have been proud to have rhymed up perhaps, but we can only be thankful that the Editor was a man of some insight who recognised the foundations of a towering talent.

Although much of his early work inevitably targeted wartime issues, it was underpinned by the basics of that mischievous, leg-cawing brand of Glasgow humour which he made his trademark. Classic nuggets of Neill's style of Glaswegian humour began to punctuate the *Evening Times* pages. The readers recognised themselves in Bud's wee drawings and pithy one-liners and they laughed.

Unlike most of his contemporaries in newspaper cartooning, Bud's early drawing style and approach to his subjects was heavily influenced by American newspaper artists like George McManus (Bringing Up Father), EC Segar (Popeye), Rudolf Dirks (Katzenjammer Kids), Bud Fisher (Mutt & Jeff) and the zany Bill Holman (Smokey Stover). Bud had stayed in Canada for a year just before the war and had been exposed to a daily diet of the energetic and fresh artwork which appeared in *"The Funnies"* page of the national papers. These popular strips had subject matters which ranged from fantastical science fiction adventures to everyday domestic family situations.

The British pocket cartoon origins were derived from Hogarth's heavily cross-hatched engravings and, later, Thomas Rowlandson and James Gillray's satirical pen and ink drawings which lampoooned establishment figures of the day. The cartoon strip was almost exclusively aimed at the young in periodical comic form.

In contrast, the American cartoon strip and pocket cartoon had developed into a sophisticated and dynamic art form which was avidly read by both young and old in the daily newspapers.

The root of this dynamism was quintissentially American - "the Mighty Dollar". National newspaper magnates like Hearst and Pulitzer realised at a relatively early stage in cartoon art's development that it could be used as a powerful selling tool in the battle for readership. Popular strips and their creators were head-hunted with substantial monetary incentives and working conditions and imbued with 'star' status. The best of these strips had an economical style, an animated pace and a degree of sophistication that was totally lacking in its British counterpart.

Ever curious, Bud experimented with drawing styles and techniques throughout his career, particularly in his pocket cartoons.

The earlier *Evening Times* cartoons were closer in style to his American cartoonist mentors' work. When he left the *Times* for the *Daily Record*, his artwork had become self-assured and it had gelled into the robust, yet elegant style that he had made his own. His line was cleaner. The frame was economically filled, yet full of detail.

Bud's cartoon heroes and heroines, the wee Hughies and Mrs T's of his world had a three-dimensional earthiness. The not-so-wee inked wimmen looked all of their "3oz, 12lb and 18 stane" and the smell of greetin'-faced weans' stale nappies was almost palpable. You felt you had met them before, based as they were on the ordinary city people whose spirit and feistiness gave, (and still give), Glasgow its unique identity. Bud caught them in his frame and with the unique voice he had developed, allowed us to eavesdrop on his Neillian gems.

A further change of newspaper heralded another development in Bud's drawing style. The *Express* cartoons became masterly pen and ink drawings. Minimal lines, just this side of describing form were anchored by blocks and blobs of black ink. His gag lines became subtler, at times almost obscure. With this minimalist drawing style, he had reached the zenith of his cartoon art craft - virtuoso renditions of line, form and balance.

In what were to be his last five years, Bud, ever the creative artist, experimented with "cameraless photography" as he dubbed it, using an assortment of nuts, bolts and screws etc. as his cartoon characters, sculptural pieces and his own versions of the Rorschach ink blot test.

These inventive and innovative artworks were an indication of Bud's intention to explore new forms and approaches to his cartoon art and had he lived his three score and ten who knows what delights would have awaited us in our daily paper.

Going through my archives of Bud Neill's work for this volume was, as it always is, a great pleasure, a tonic and antidote to the prosaic in life. I trust this collection will brighten up your day.

Finally, I would like to thank Yvonne Barron who worked with me on the painstaking task of restoring Bud's newsprinted artwork, (regrettably few originals exist, therefore most of the cartoons in this book have been sourced from ageing, poor quality newspaper cuttings). I am also grateful for the assistance and cooperation of the Neill family, Maria Somerville, the *Evening Times*, the *Daily Record* and the *Scottish Daily Express*.

Ranald MacColl
Glasgow, 1997

THE WAR

"They tell me yon yin Hitler's a richt bad rascal an' a' . . ."

"And to what do you attribute your
phenomenal success as a fighter pilot ?"

"Sure we're war criminals, Slug, but don't worry.
If they try us in Glasgow it will be a ten-bob fine."

"My, but yir boat's a real wee treat, son. Jist like a new pin, aye. Hiv ye a wummun comes in?"

"Your orders are to drive a wedge into the Allied flanks.
I'll send a man along to help you."

"If ye ask me, they'll never catch him. He'll tak' yin o' his
Luftywuffy airyplanes and scram tae Thibet or Edinbury . . ."

"I'm not fussy about size.
It's just for throwing in the air on V-day . . ."

"Then, as if things wusnae bad enough a'ready,
the bloomin' war has got tae go an' feenish."

THE RATIONS

"Onythin' succulent for a greetin'-faced
carnivore jist in fae his work?"

"Perhaps if you look in tomorrow.
Our cat will be out tonight again."

"Pilfering of the country's food stocks has now reached alarming proportions." - News Item.

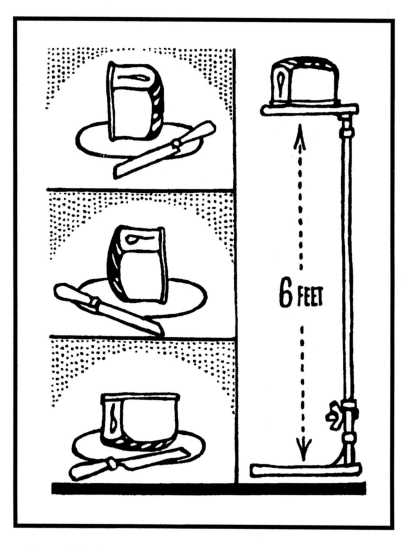

**Three delightful novel ways of serving dinner tonight,
and a suggestion for a dainty high tea.**

"Purely for display purposes, madam.
We blew them up with a bicycle pump."

"I kent whit I'd like fae Santy this year, Hughie.
Wan o' the hin' legs aff his reindeer."

GI BRIDES

"Gie's a jug o' somethin' diabolical, hen. I've a date wi' a Yank."

"You would go an' mairry an' Alasky felly, an' Cathie up the sterr gawn oot tae Hollywoood wi' jist a bathin' suit an' saun-shoes."

"Apart fae onythin' else, hingin' aboot here is haudin'
up wee Calvin's eddication somethin' terrible -
an' him comin' oot tae be a cowboy tae."

"Nellie's man's got a job in Californy noo
wi' somebody the name o' Al Catraz . . ."

"Mind o' yon Blackfeet Indian G.I. Jessie went oot tae
America tae marry? Right imposter, so he wus.
Turned oot his feet's no' ony blacker than Jessie's . . ."

"Turned oot tae be wan' o' thae Blackfeet Indians.
Ast me tae stey in a wiggy-wam in Arizony -
an' me wi' ma guid claes on, tae."

FERRS PLEEZ

"9.55. Well, aff we go again, Nellie - hurtlin' through the night wi' wur precious cargo o' human lives."

"Can ye no' unnerstaun' English? There's nae dugs gets
on the caurs unless they're no' Alsations, an' there's
nane at a' gets on if there's wan up the sterr a'ready."

"I Dream O' Jeannie Wi' The Light Brow-wown Herr . . .
wan inside an' two up the sterr."

"Yideef? I said the caur's flippin' flup . . ."

"Fae my experience, thae bus drivers wi' their hats
bent intae the shape o' a Nazi general's is the
worst on the road - an' if they've a Ronald Colman
moustache alang wi't, haud on for yir life."

"For Whom the Bell Tolls - and tolls and tolls and tolls."

BAUCHLES, BAIRNS AND BAMS

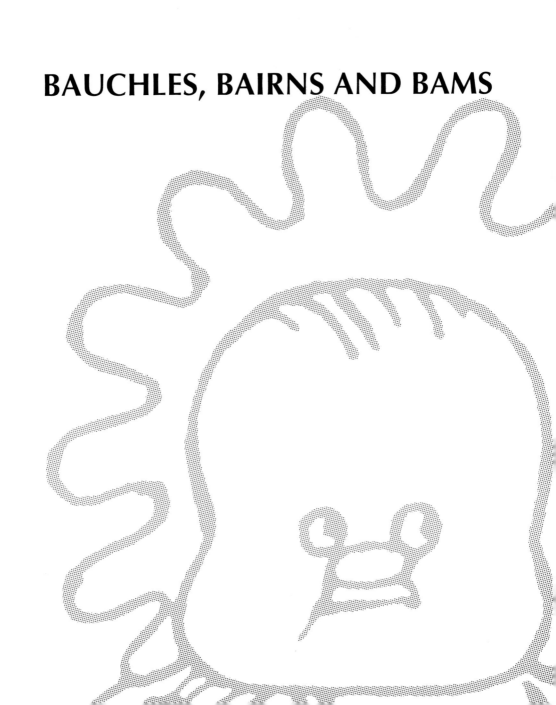

"Maybe his china's no' workin'."

"There'll likely be an awfy rammy when the bloke
comes back, Nellie, but we'll jist staun' wur grun'."

"An awfy length o' a picture, so it is. Whitever it was that
went wi' the wind took aboot fower 'oors tae go . . ."

"Here comes auld Daisy again. Some day she'll
maybe get the hang o' that pressure cooker . . ."

"Well, I widnae jist say ye're as bad as that,
Mac, but ye're certainly nae ile paintin' . . ."

"Hiv a wee rummie aboot an' see if the budgie's in there . . ."

"It's his teeth, aye. Awfy crabbit. Like a bear wi' nae fags."

"Great how the years slip in. Another
three weeks and I'll be 10 months."

"He's gettin' teeth. Feel . . ."

"Shuggy was expectin' an Injun outfit, but noo we'll
jist hiv tae play at Cowboys an' Bus Conductors . . ."

"Is that right whit the weans was tellin' me the noo?
Nae Santa Claus?"

"Nae kiddin'. I seen ye the meenit I saw ye . . ."

"Awfy clever wean, this. Say 'Awa' an' bile yir
heid' that ye learnt aff the budgie, hen . . ."

**Portrait of Mrs Thomson officially opening
the Toonheid windae-hingin' season.**

NINE TO FIVE

"Good afternoon, madam - and what
can I do for you, o-boy-o-boy-o-boy?"

"You can knock away the props now, Charlie. It's sold."

"Crikey! Our Glengoggy instructress has started a clan war by patching the seat of a Campbell kilt with MacDonald tartan."

"Good afternoon. Have you a high-powered,
long, low, black saloon car?"

"Stick 'em up - and no tricks."

"See's a light, Mac . . ."

DOON THE WATTER

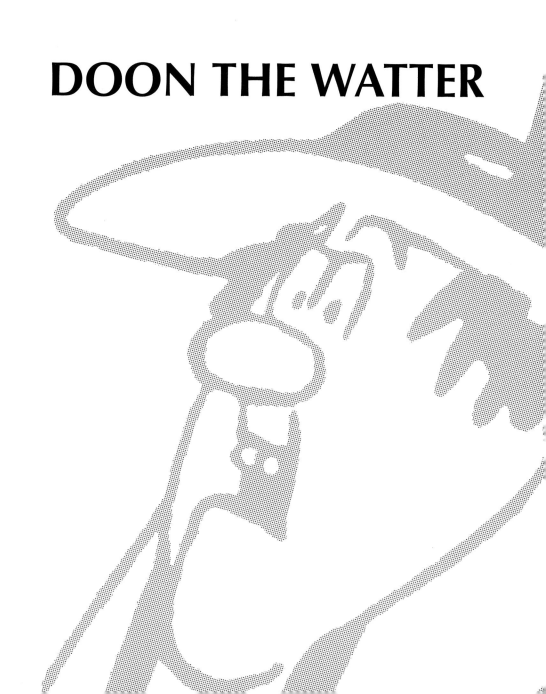

"There Jessie awa' in a dook. The Firth o' Clyde's
gonnae get an awfy hammerin' . . ."

"My, but I like rid herr. Rid herr's rerr."

"You come oot the watter this meenit, ye bad wee rascal, or I'll ring yir ear tae ye! Ye wantin' knockit doon wi' a battleship?"

"'Tis truly said that the sea holds some fearsome secrets."

"Nellie's went an' stepped on wan o'
thae wee squiggly things again."

"Spent five quid on ma New Look hat, tae, an'
the only thing that's whustled efter me since I
came doon tae this dump's been seagulls . . ."

"Yaffayat? Whityatyaffa?"

SPORTSLINE

"Right . . . . this time."

"Here's a parachute, Charlie, in case you have to bale out."

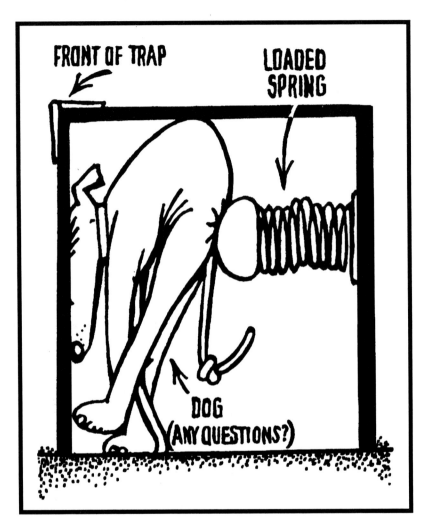

The Bud Neill Spring Booster for slow-trapping greyhounds.
Patent applied for.

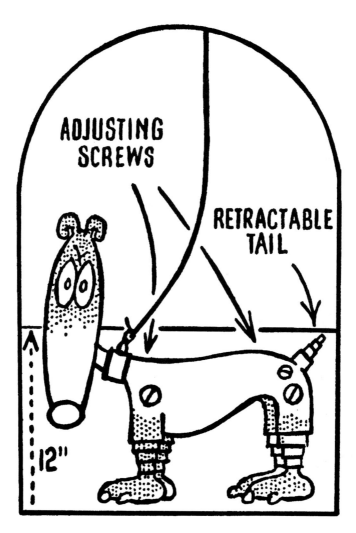

By crossing a greyhound with a telescope, Sportsline Kennels have at last evolved this racing dog which can be shoved under bus and railway carriage seats.

"Now, that's what I call a GOAL."

Spot The Ball competition. No large cash prizes offered.

WEE WIMMEN AND WEE MEN

"Oor Jessie's confined tae the hoose wi' a
home perm she made a mistake wi' . . ."

"92 - an' that's him awa' tae buy a refill for his ball-pen."

"Terrible faddy. She likes jelly babies but she's no'
awfy stuck on the heids."

"See they've snaw'n ice. 'Snaw nice, snaw'n ice."

"Hello Mrs Todd, an' whit are ye near deid wi' this morning?"

"If I wis tae wear that ma knees
wid hiv a nervous breakdown . . ."

"Very neatly did. All I have to dae noo is
learn to bend my elbows the ither way."

"Sure, we've a washin' machine. I'm it . . ."

"An' here's a sort o' bookcase thing I
knocked together from odds an' ends."

"That's Bessie's on the top.
Wi' the edelweiss in the windae box . . ."

"Talk aboot murder?
The palms o' ma feet's got slipped discs next . . ."

"I'm 3oz, 12lb, an' 18 stane . . ."

WIMMEN AND WEANS

"I'll no' be sorry when they're a' oot workin' . . ."

"Drink yir milk or ye'll no' grow up tae be a lazy,
shiftless auld lay-aboot like yir Daddy!"

"If onyone's askin' - I'm baskin'."

"Careful, son. General Nelson lost his e'e squintin' through wan o' them things at the Battle o' Bannockburn . . ."

"I'm no' right sure, son, but I suppose
they'll eat snaw an' stuff . . ."

"Awfy versatile wean. He murders the mandolin an' all . . ."

MRS T

"Mrs. Thomson should be along ony meenit noo . . ."

"Peep, peep, peepin' their horns, tae. Couldnae hear a word Mrs. Thomson was sayin' when we stopped for a wee blether on a zebra crossing . . ."

"A couple o' vodkas don't hauf murder Mrs. Thomson's decorum, don't they, Mrs. T?"

"Mrs. Thomson's fur hat escaped fae Russia durin'
the Revolution, didn't it, Mrs. Thomson?"

"Mrs. Thomson disnae think it'll thaw till the
weather gets warmer, dae ye, Mrs. Thomson?"

"If there's wan thing Mrs. Thomson is,
it's optimistic, in't it, Mrs. T.?"

THE MESSAGES

"He hisnae left oot ony tomatties for squeezin' the day . . ."

"Ye don't hauf hear some rumours. A wumman was jist tellin'
me there's mair fush in the sea than ever came oot o't . . ."

"Raw mince . . . it aye looks awfy SAIR."

"Bit o' a comic, him. Gie's me dugfish
for the cat an' catfish for the dug . . ."

"Here's a couple o' things tae test yir powers o' invention . . ."

"I've aye meant tae ask ye . . .
is thae things hingin' up wee coos?"

LIPSTICK AND LUMBERS

"Whit's all the panic aboot? Haud yir horses
till I feenish lusciousin' ma lips . . ."

"Who d'ye think ye was whustlin' efter, I hope?"

"Is that no' dreary? Ma flippin' bouffant's boofed . . ."

"I'm no jivin' this wan, Mac.
I've jist new regained ma poise . . ."

"Mine'sis faither's got a ranch on Broadway . . ."

"She's loyal - I'll say that for her.
She's held on tae him a' winter . . ."

TEDS

"Ye're a marvel, Toamy. Hoo d'ye manage tae get
that air o' studied carelessness intae yir attire?"

"Bang him wan wi' yir coiffure, Toamy . . ."

"C'mon we'll see wur lawyer. Here a bloke sayin' maist
Teddy boys is neat, clean an' well-mannered . . ."

"Toamy's an individualist . . ."

"Big Toamy commitit social suicide in the barber's this mornin'.
Short at the back and sides . . ."

"It otty be a National Ishy, sur.
Upholstered street corners fur the boys, sur . . ."

CAURS AND CLIPPIES

"Glesca's aboot the only city in Britain whaur ye'll
see a tram car bashin' aboot in its wild state."

"Noo we'll try it together.
Deep breath . . . chest oot . . . FERZ PULEEZ!"

"Tryin' tae make us look like a
lot of flippin' lassies, so they are . . ."

"It's san-ferry-ann tae me whether he knocked yir teeth in or no', Mac. There's still nae spittin' on the caurs . . . "

"If every tram in Glesca was laid end tae end alang Argyle Street at the rush 'oor, it widnae be nothin' oot the usual."

"Aw, Jimmy! There's a wee wumman
wants aff upstairs if ye've a meenit . . ."

THE POLIS

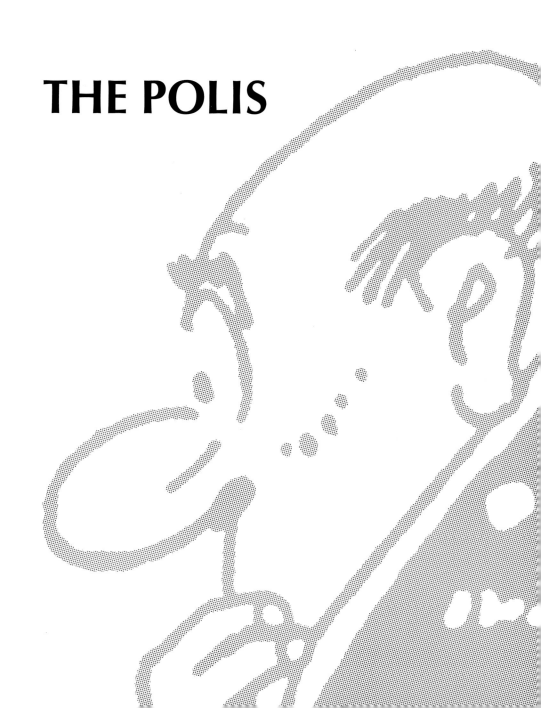

"Ye don't hauf see some sinister-lookin'
polis floatin' aboot these days . . . "

"Now, the smart caper here, probationer, is tae wander roon' the corner till somebody reports it . . ."

"Ma man's disappeared but this is no'
in the nature o' a complaint, like . . ."

"Ye'll no' hiv found a big yelly dug aboot this size that'd take
the haun' aff ye as soon's look at ye, I don't suppose naw?"

"Bloke 'ae see ye, Ina. Aboot five six,
ruddy complexion, leer on top lip . . ."

"Ye'll no' hiv saw a lost wean cried Wullie wi' nae breeks an' a runnin' nose aboot this high?"

ARRAFERR

"Ye cannae get a cairry, son. Yir mither's full up . . ."

"Move ower a wee bit, son - ye're staunin' in ma light."

"A DOUBLE nuggit? Ye don't hiv tae go mad . . ."

"Oh, I see, aye. The faster ye flap them two bits
o' widd aboot, the quicker the boat hurries . . ."

"Will ye manage?"

"Aboot time we were gettin' ashore.
We've been bletherin' long enough . . ."

FISH AND FAUNA

"Hoo d'ye get tae the Pacific fae here, Mac?"

"Did I no' see ye on a Christmas card, mate?"

"This your dug?"

"Oot wi' the boys, I suppose - an'
me sittin' over a hot egg all day."

"Ye look great the noo - aboot five-bob-a-pound."

"Pey nae attention. He's gettin' a terrible show-aff . . ."

"He's a kind o' small miniature a some breed o' wee dugs . . ."

"Pay nae attention - he only snaps if
he thinks ye're frightened o' him."

TERASSIN' AND TEARS

"Well, which terracin' dae ye propose keepin'
in stitches the day wi' yir witty asides?"

"Psychic, this wan. Kent I wis fae Glesca
afore I even opened ma mooth . . ."

**A fine action study of Wearies' versatile goalkeeper,
tensed in readiness to let through another six.**

"That's oor big centre's day made, noo.
He got a kick at the ba' . . ."

"Efter this, the bools'll seem a harum-
scarum, tearaway gemme . . ."

"A bloke tae see ye. Says he's a mate o' yon
wee referee ye were roarin' at on Saturday!"

EXPRESS VIEWS

"Aberdeen says its the storms . . . . . ."

"Okay, lads, drop everything and send our mighty slicer roaring into a nerve-tingling crescendo of shattering action - here comes Mrs. Mac for her weekly ounce of streaky."

"Flying will hold no terrors for me, young man. For thirty years
I've been cleaning windows on a pair of shuggly three-legged
steps which would daunt even Douglas Bader . . . . . ."

"Whitehall will be fizzin'. I hear that
Pertick's declarin' itself a Republic."

"They tell me the Government is now proposing a penny-a-year
licence for budgerigars which would bring in an annual
fifty-million-quid from Knightswood alone . . . . . ."

On the Capital's Rose Street Beat we spotted this Serbian Nose Flautist resting before a concert.

"I'd like a job of some responsibility and authority, some vocation in which my decisions would not be arbitrarily dismissed as the rantings of an idiot. I'm a first division football referee."

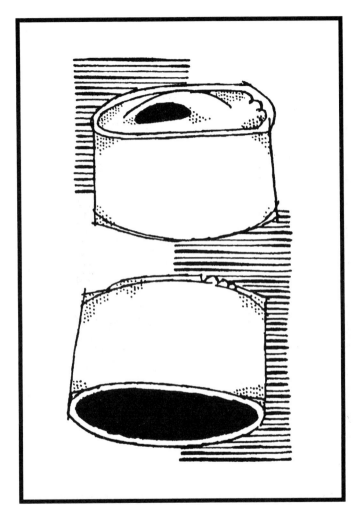

Because of meat prices, pies will be dearer.
An alternative would be to eliminate that ridiculous wee
hole in the top and put a great big hole in the bottom.